ALDERSGATE SPECIAL NEEDS MINISTRY: 2003-2023

The First Twenty Years

Lovingly compiled by current and former trustees
of Aldersgate Special Needs Ministry

Twenty-Year History Committee Chair: Susan Hasty Kovas

Edited by Emily and Daly Ward

Interviews by Mimi Sizemore

South Carolina United Methodist Advocate Press

Copyright © 2023 by South Carolina United Methodist Advocate Press

Scripture quotations marked (NIV) are taken from The Holy Bible, New International Version, Copyright © 1973, 1978, 1984 by the International Bible Society. THE HOLY BIBLE, NEW INTERNATIONAL VERSION®, NIV® Copyright © 1973, 1978, 1984, 2011 by Biblica, Inc.® Used by permission. All rights reserved worldwide.

Scripture quotations marked (ESV) are taken from The Holy Bible, English Standard Version. ESV® Text Edition: 2016. Copyright © 2001 by Crossway, a publishing ministry of Good News Publishers. Used by permission. All rights reserved.

"The United Methodist Hymnal: Book of United Methodist Worship." Nashville, Tenn. The United Methodist Publishing House, 1989.

All rights reserved. No part of this book may be reproduced or transmitted in any form or by any means, electronic or mechanical, including photocopying, recording or by any information storage and retrieval system, without permission in writing from the Publisher.

First published in the United States of America in 2023
by the South Carolina United Methodist Advocate Press.

Library of Congress Cataloging-in-Publication Data
Aldersgate Special Needs Ministry: 2003-2023
p. cm.

Cover photo: Matt Brodie

ISBN 979-8-9883575-3-7

"My people will live in peaceful dwelling places, in secure homes, in undisturbed places of rest."—Isaiah 32:18 (NIV)

Aldersgate Special Needs Ministry is a fully self-sustaining, not-for-profit organization affiliated with the South Carolina Conference of The United Methodist Church. Formed in 2003 by family and friends seeking residential solutions for loved ones with developmental disabilities, Aldersgate's mission is to provide Christian homes with the highest quality of life and greatest level of independence for adults with special needs.

All Aldersgate homes are located near Christian communities for the purpose of giving residents a sense of God-inspired inclusion and interaction.

Providing Homes of Grace and Love

410 Harbison Blvd., Columbia, SC 29212
P.O. Box 203, Ballentine, SC 29002
803-590.4890 • AldersgateSNM.org

Tom Hering (left) and his parents, Yvette and Rich Hering, bowled regularly with the Fun Strikers, a group of families with special needs children who got together often for fellowship and fun at Anchor Lanes Bowling Alley in Irmo, South Carolina. Out of their friendship arose the idea for Aldersgate Special Needs Ministry.

Preface

God moves in a mysterious way
His wonders to perform;
He plants his footsteps in the sea
and rides upon the storm.
"God Moves in a Mysterious Way"—William Cowper (1774)

Yvette Hering held her gaze as she studied lane #3 at Anchor Lanes Bowling Alley in Irmo, South Carolina. A bowling alley is definitely not a metaphor for life, Yvette thought as she smiled to herself. Here, smooth, flat, polished lanes form a straight path. Avoid the gutters and the rest is easy: no curves, no bumps, no ups, and certainly no downs.

But life is not like a bowling alley.

Yvette and her husband, Rich, along with son Tom, bowled regularly in the late 1990s with good friends in the Columbia area. It was great fun, especially for Tom and his buddies who delighted in each roll, laughed at every wobbly pin, and howled at the occasional gutter ball. Unmindful of time and scores, it was simply good friends laughing and being together.

Bowling was their passion, but the love of the game was not the common thread that brought these friends together. Their bond had nothing to do with strikes or spares.

+++

Most families experience the generation-to-generation life cycles and stages that God intended. A child is born, loved, nurtured, and taught to live independently. As the child ages and becomes an adult, parental guidance is tenderly and intentionally withdrawn with the new adult achieving independence and self-sufficiency. This natural progression is repeated over and over as the wheel of life spins on.

But long-term independence and self-reliance are not attained by everyone, especially when certain special children become adults. In the 1990s, intellectual and developmental disabilities made independent living impossible for nearly three thousand adults in South Carolina, most of whom were middle-aged and remained at home with aging parents who were struggling with the double responsibility of caring for themselves and their handicapped adult children.

The "children" in the bowling group were among those three thousand South Carolinians with disabilities. All were now adults, and all lived with aging caregivers. Every mom and dad in the bowling group was shouldering the same enormous load of parental concern: Not one of these young adults was capable of living independently, and no family had a workable plan for the future.

Turning to one another for support and guidance, these parents shared worries and questions. Where will my child with disabilities live when I am no longer able to provide care? Will quality, loving attention be rendered? Why are there not enough residential options for adults with special needs in South Carolina?

An uncertain future for a vulnerable loved one causes apprehension, and even fear, for parents.

For the Wednesday evening bowling group, the time had come to do more than knock down pins. It was time to knock on doors.

Yvette and Rich Hering with their son, Tom, helped found Aldersgate. As aging caregivers, they worried what would happen to Tom if they couldn't care for him at home any longer.

The Herings wanted to ensure their son, Tom—who was not capable of living independently because of his special needs—would always have a loving home.

Chapter 1

PUNCH TIME

Come, Holy Spirit, come;
Let thy bright beams arise;
Dispel the darkness from our minds,
And open all our eyes.
"Come, Holy Spirit, Come"—Joseph Hart (1759)

As purpose and mission began to gel for the Herings and their band of like-minded friends, so did their organization. A name was adopted, PUNCH (Parents United for Needed Choice in Housing), and the group swelled as new members were identified and added. Typical channels for recruiting included neighbors, church members, a "friend of a friend," and anyone with a connection to an adult with special needs and concerns about the future. All were welcome.

Early meetings at Grace United Methodist Church in Columbia, South Carolina, generated more questions than answers for reversing the residential availability issue.

Should we build a home ourselves? If so, how would we operate it? What funding sources are available? Do we approach government agencies for ideas and partnering?

Can we even do this?

One particular strategy session in the Grace sanctuary steered PUNCH members toward a compelling idea: Perhaps there was a South Carolina church or religious organization that would be interested in adopting this urgent need as an outreach ministry.

With this one inspiration, everything was about to change.

The PUNCH group approached a variety of churches and denominations. Only the South Carolina Conference of The United Methodist Church returned the call. The rest is divine history.

Chapter 2

DEGREES OF SEPARATION

*O for a thousand tongues to sing
my great Redeemer's praise,
the glories of my God and King,
the triumphs of his grace!*
"O for a Thousand Tongues to Sing"—Charles Wesley (1739)

In early 2002, with a preliminary although undefined response from the South Carolina United Methodist Church, PUNCH members were feeling hopeful. Perhaps momentum might be turning slightly in their favor.

One hundred thirty miles to the east on the Charleston coast, another South Carolina family impacted by the special needs housing crisis was not as optimistic.

Judy and Arden Weathers and daughter Laura of Orangeburg, South Carolina, were vacationing at the Isle of Palms in January 2002. The Weathers family had many warm memories from family beach vacations, but this trip was different. Laura now lived several states away at a school that could help meet her special needs. The family did not like being apart, and Laura's return to Kentucky at the end of the week loomed large and painful.

Hungarian writer Frigyes Karinthy famously theorized that each of us on the planet is separated by only "six degrees" or six social connections. South Carolina is apparently the proving ground for his theory. Stir in the far-reaching United Methodist network, our small state ("don't I know you?"), and a chance meeting on the beach, and those six degrees of separation vanish.

At the Isle of Palms it was the dead of winter, but warm enough on that particular January day for the Weathers family to take a walk on the beach. While the family strolled, a figure approached with a familiar gait and a big smile. Nancy Ayers, their former Orangeburg neighbor, was walking toward them. Ayers had watched Laura grow up and was keenly aware of the family's situation.

Old friends exchanged embraces and relayed family happenings, but it was Ayers who had huge news that would completely change the course of the Weathers family's journey.

+ + +

Nancy Ayers

Ayers explained to the Weathers family that a movement was afoot to energize the South Carolina Conference of The United Methodist Church to more fully utilize conference properties, such as land that could be used for something desperately needed: residential alternatives for adults with special needs.

Even more enticing, one such prospect was in the Weathers' and Ayers' backyard. The Oaks was an Orangeburg area retirement facility on a sprawling campus with ample land and a forward-thinking chief executive officer. The Oaks would make an ideal place to explore building homes for adults with disabilities.

Less than two months later, the Weathers family was in the office of the Reverend James McGee, president of The Oaks, exchanging ideas as to how a unique partnership between The Oaks and families in need might work. Ayers and The Oaks CEO, Johnnie Benson, also attended the formative meeting.

Much work needed to be done before construction could even be discussed. But most importantly, God had converged two paths to the same small point on a South Carolina beach. Inertia was finally broken and hope prevailed.

An entity within South Carolina United Methodism still needed to be planned and created, then recognized and approved, not only by the governing body of The Oaks, but also by the United Methodist Conference itself. Guided by Rev. McGee and Ayers, progress continued in early 2002 as pieces began to align.

Chapter 3

IN THE BEGINNING

*Angels from the realms of glory,
wing your flight o'er all the earth;
ye who sang creation's story
now proclaim Messiah's birth.*
"Angels From the Realms of Glory"—James Montgomery (1816)

By the summer of 2002, the Weathers family, the Herings, PUNCH families, and others were working together and justifiably encouraged. A September 2002 meeting had been scheduled with a highly regarded leader of the Board of Health and Welfare, an influential arm of the South Carolina Conference of The United Methodist Church. As God, not luck, would have it, that leader was Health and Welfare Board Chair Nancy Ayers. Ayers had become passionate about the growing shortfall in housing for the disabilities and special needs community and was ready to hear more from a broader audience of families.

At the same time, someone else was watching the progress of this effort with great interest. J. Lawrence McCleskey, bishop of the South Carolina Conference of The United Methodist Church since 1996, had come to South Carolina from Charlotte, North Carolina, where United Methodists in the Western North Carolina Conference had been operating group homes and apartments for special needs adults since the early 1980s.

On September 10, 2002, a very warm Tuesday morning at Conference Center headquarters in Columbia, South Carolina, Ayers met with Al and Beth Austin, Faye Jackson, Judy Weathers, the Reverend James McGee, Yvette and Rich Hering, Al and Pricilla Raymond, Daly Ward, Johnnie Benson, and others. Later that month, on September 28, a formal proposal to create a task force was presented to the full Board of Health and Welfare in Greenwood, South Carolina.

The request was overwhelmingly approved. God had breathed life into a new United Methodist entity charged with developing a comprehensive ministry for the purpose of building and operating residential opportunities for South Carolina adults with special needs.

Yvette Hering described her feelings about these meetings as "daunting, but very thankful for the support and guidance from the conference, the representatives from the Board of Health and Welfare, and several United Methodist pastors who were willing to be involved in helping begin this ministry." The newly approved task force would operate under the umbrella of The United Methodist Church as an agency of the South Carolina Conference.

"It wasn't difficult to get support because anyone who had a loved one with special needs would say 'yes' to it," commented Bishop McCleskey.

Indeed, demonstrating the need was effortless. Explaining the cause was simple. Building the ministry would prove to be a far greater challenge.

Chapter 4

WHAT'S IN A NAME?

To serve the present age, my calling to fulfill;
O may it all my powers engage to do my Master's will!
"A Charge to Keep I Have"—Charles Wesley (1762)

By the fall of 2002, the task force was operating as a fully sanctioned organization within the conference and a slate of members was drafted. The founding group included Nancy Ayers, Richard and Yvette Hering, Faye Jackson, Margaret McCleskey, Rev. James McGee, Al and Priscilla Raymond, Rev. Harry Stullenbarger, Rev. Stephen Taylor, Daly Ward, Arden and Judy Weathers, and others.

Now a viable United Methodist organization, the task force considered an appropriate name for the ministry. By definition, a task force is temporary. Once the "task" is complete, the "force" disbands, but there was nothing temporary or transitory about this ministry or the people behind it.

The ministry needed a permanent, substantive name with Methodist origins. Rev. McGee suggested the name should acknowledge the United Methodist heritage and affiliation. "Aldersgate," he pointed out, is synonymous with the founder of Methodism, John Wesley.

While attending a prayer meeting in 1738 on Aldersgate Street in London, Wesley's heart was "strangely warmed." It was Aldersgate Street where Wesley experienced a new capacity to trust in Christ with the faith of a child. "Aldersgate" was immediately embraced as the perfect moniker for this new initiative.

With name selected and members in place, the next charge was to receive formal South Carolina Conference approval at the next Annual Conference. This occurred in May 2003, at the Annual Conference held at Wofford College, Spartanburg,

South Carolina. Two months later on July 18, 2003, at conference headquarters in Columbia, Aldersgate founders met for the last time as a task force. Symbolically adjourning the meeting, they immediately reconvened as a fully authorized Board of Trustees for Aldersgate Special Needs Ministry. Weathers was elected chair, Rev. Taylor as vice-chair, Hering as secretary, and Al Austin as treasurer.

The long organization process was finally complete when Aldersgate secured not-for-profit, tax-exempt status as a South Carolina entity and legally incorporated in December 2003.

Now the real work could begin.

Bishop J. Lawrence McCleskey and his wife, Margaret Fowler McCleskey, were heavily involved with the founding of Aldersgate Special Needs Ministry. Margaret had been the director of development for UMAR, a housing provider for adults with intellectual disabilities in North Carolina, and she brought much needed expertise and guidance to the team.

Chapter 5

HITCHES AND HURDLES, GIFTS AND ANGELS

Teach me some melodious sonnet,
sung by flaming tongues above
Praise the mount! I'm fixed upon it,
mount of thy redeeming love!
"Come, Thou Fount of Every Blessing"—Robert Robinson (1758)

    The new trustees had much to learn and were eager to begin. Nearly every other United Methodist Conference in the Southeast was already actively engaged in a special needs housing ministry. The South Carolina Conference was years behind.
    That's when God graced Aldersgate with two gifts that would prove priceless: a dynamic, Christian leader with special needs housing experience and a friendly neighbor with a respected record in group home management.
    An adjacent United Methodist conference, the Western North Carolina Conference, had an established history as a housing provider for adults with intellectual disabilities. UMAR, headquartered in Charlotte, North Carolina, had been successfully building homes for persons with developmental disabilities since the early 1980s.
    By heavenly coincidence, Margaret Fowler McCleskey, wife of Bishop McCleskey, was the former director of development for UMAR. She was one of the principal reasons for UMAR's growth to more than twenty group homes and apartments in central and western North Carolina. Best of all, she was willing to join Aldersgate in management, board, and development roles.
    Daly Ward had served WNC-UMAR as a trustee in the 1980s. He remarked, "I was delighted to work with Margaret again. She was the ideal person at the perfect time for Aldersgate Special Needs Ministry."

McCleskey coached and guided as UMAR shared resources and Aldersgate trustees navigated their way through the arduous effort to obtain state licensure, find sites, and break ground.

Aldersgate eventually learned that North Carolina red tape is not the same as South Carolina red tape. Differing regulations between the two states required that Aldersgate move forward without following the UMAR model. This was a setback but also an opportunity for prayer and discernment.

There would be an abundance of both in the months ahead.

+ + +

In the early years, Aldersgate's exposure to South Carolina United Methodism circles was very limited. Trustees were mindful that their largely invisible ministry needed to increase awareness if Aldersgate were to raise capital and transcend from a mere dream to real rooftops.

As Faye Jackson, one of the founding trustees, stated, "We were confident that we could lease land and find money for home construction, but we knew the real challenge was to come up with the funds to staff, furnish, and operate the homes." Yvette Hering added that navigating the maze of multiple state agencies to access and obtain licensing was also a test for the new ministry.

Hering summarized the challenge, "We were the new ministry in the Conference and struggling to make ourselves known."

Rev. Stephen Taylor added, "Neither I nor anyone else knew what to do because Aldersgate was a group of individuals with a vision, but no experience in marketing a unique organization like ours."

The board's aptitude for marketing was better than they realized. An insightful trustee approached Rev. Taylor with some delightful work by a talented young local artist. The paintings of angels were captivating in their simplicity and charm. Rev. Taylor immediately realized he was looking at the foundation for a solid campaign to raise awareness and a flow of capital for Aldersgate.

Slightly plump and complete with halo and wings, the happy, grinning angels radiated love and joy. Aldersgate Angels became the first campaign of the young ministry. In exchange for a financial commitment, a contributor would receive a colorful Aldersgate Angel lapel pin. The promotion raised much-needed funds, and Rev. Taylor modestly explained, "We were very pleased with the success of the first campaign."

Aldersgate Angels immediately raised consciousness, but other positive forces were also at work.

Never underestimate the power of the good word, especially when it comes from

Tom Hering (right) shows Bishop J. Lawrence McCleskey how to play a handheld video game. Hering was one of many special needs adults who stood to benefit from the Aldersgate Special Needs Ministry.

a United Methodist pulpit. A growing band of conference ministers began preaching about Aldersgate and spreading the ministry's inspiring story. Aldersgate Sunday was incubated from this nucleus of supporters and has since become a permanent part of the conference's August calendar. Boosted by encouragement from Bishop McCleskey, and later Bishop Mary Virginia Taylor and Bishop L. Jonathan Holston, the mention of Aldersgate Special Needs Ministry began to draw fewer blank stares and more smiles of recognition.

Chapter 6

A SPADE IS TURNED—A HOME IS UNDER WAY!

Unresting, unhasting, and silent as light,
nor wanting, nor wasting, thou rulest in might;
thy justice like mountains high soaring above
thy clouds, which are fountains of goodness and love.
"Immortal, Invisible, God Only Wise"—Walter C. Smith (1867)

The inaugural step in any journey is the most challenging. The same can be said of the first project when launching a special needs housing ministry. "Don't reinvent the wheel" may be conventional wisdom, but for Aldersgate, the wheel did not even exist in South Carolina.

The Weathers family, Nancy Ayers, Rev. James McGee, and others in Orangeburg continued to chisel away at The Oaks project, working diligently and praying that the shape of a home would soon take form.

At the same time, the board was exploring the possibility of a second ground lease site to complement the Orangeburg project. After months of searching for location number two, Aldersgate trustees realized that God's intervention was needed if a site were to be found.

An idea had been circulating that perhaps an Aldersgate home could be constructed on another United Methodist property, and an excellent prospect was only a few miles from conference headquarters. Thanks to the efforts and planning of many, a much beloved sister ministry came through for Aldersgate in a generous way.

Epworth Children's Home on Millwood Avenue in Columbia, also a United Methodist agency, was the gold standard in providing for children in need of care and shelter for more than a century. Perhaps Epworth would make space available

Dan Shumaker, Judy Weathers, Bishop Mary Virginia Taylor, Al Bynum and other key supporters gather March 27, 2006, for the groundbreaking of Columbia Builders Care Home, Aldersgate Special Needs Ministry's first home for special needs adults.

for another ministry with a similar vision.

On March 27, 2006, a bright, clear Monday on Epworth's east campus, seven spades ceremoniously pierced the firm, red clay, and an Aldersgate home was finally under way. Present at the groundbreaking ceremony were Aldersgate Chair Judy Weathers, Arden Weathers, South Carolina United Methodist Conference Bishop Mary Virginia Taylor, Dan Shumaker (CEO of Shumaker Homes), Al Bynum (vice chair of the Epworth Children's Home Board of Trustees), Rev. Stephen Taylor, Dr. and Mrs. McKay Brabham and daughter Margaret Brabham, Caroline Stephenson, Nancy and Harris Davis, Tammy Fulmer, Tim and Gwen Macy, Yvette and Rich Hering, Daly Ward, and many others.

+ + +

The bricks and mortar of the first home, on Columbia's Epworth campus, would become a figurative cloak of many collaborative colors and efforts.

Epworth leadership led strongly with a symbolic one-dollar-per-year land lease.

Shumaker Homes, the Home Builders Association of Greater Columbia, and dozens of skilled workers donated hundreds of hours to constructing the first Aldersgate home, which was named the "Columbia Builders Care Home." It opened in early 2009.

Soon to follow was a huge, unexpected boost from Shumaker Homes, a well-regarded residential homebuilder headquartered in nearby Irmo, South Carolina. Shumaker pledged support by contributing project management, materials, and labor and by recruiting other area contractors and subcontractors to do the same.

Fred Berry, a senior executive with Shumaker, commented, "Dan Shumaker and the Shumaker Homes family are very excited about the project, and we appreciate the opportunity the Lord has given us to participate."

Shumaker and Berry broadened their commitment by engaging the Home Builders Association of Greater Columbia (HBAGC) and its members to become partners in the endeavor. Shumaker Homes, HBAGC, and dozens of skilled workers donated hundreds of hours to the project. In honor of these efforts, the Aldersgate home at Epworth would appreciatively be named, "Columbia Builders Care Home."

+ + +

Building a special home for special people brings with it costly and special requirements. Appreciative of the enormous efforts of Shumaker and the Columbia construction community, Aldersgate still needed to raise funds to pay for furniture, fixtures, appliances, resident transportation, project finalization, and more.

Of necessity, Aldersgate trustees became Aldersgate fundraisers. Rev. Stephen Taylor, former chair, recalls, "It was a challenge because we had limited resources and no professional fundraising guidance. We had no idea where the funds would come from."

In the end, a multifaceted approach proved fruitful. This included fundraisers, grants, private donations, pledges, and contributions from various United Methodist churches.

One of the most successful events for the Builders Care home was held in 2006. Bill and Beth Best hosted an elegant reception at their Columbia home and invited guests with a heart for adults with disabilities. Caroline Stephenson, ardent advocate and parent of a child with special needs, passionately addressed the gathering. As a result, this well-attended event raised more than $25,000 for the Columbia home. Stephenson was successful again when she connected with a college sorority friend in search of a worthy cause to support. Her Kappa Kappa Gamma sister was delighted to provide a $25,000 grant to Aldersgate. Other donations came from generous people with special needs loved ones and from caring churches across the state.

By late 2008, construction of the Columbia home was complete, and the home

Parents and guardians of future Aldersgate residents—A. McKay Brabham III (left), Ron Kuebler, Margot Kuebler, H. Edward Freeman Jr., and John McDermott—prepare to give progress reports at a board meeting on when their loved ones will be able to move into their home on the Epworth campus and Aldersgate at The Oaks.

The Columbia Builders Care Home, located on the campus of Epworth Children's Home, houses six women. Quickly after they moved into their new home, in early 2009, they endeared themselves to the community with their church involvement, hardworking attitude, and volunteerism. Above, the women gather for a meal. Below is one of the women's bedrooms.

Residents of the Columbia Builders Care Home enjoy their garden.

was ready for its first occupants. A group of future residents had already been identified and were able to participate in the December 15, 2008, ribbon cutting. Stephenson described it as a wonderful celebration made extra special because the participating residents had already gotten to know each other and were very excited to be independent and living together.

In early 2009, six thoroughly ecstatic young women moved into the Columbia Builders Care Home. Over the next few months they quickly endeared themselves to the Columbia community. Active in church, in their jobs, at Epworth, and in many volunteer areas of the community, the women of the Columbia home were embraced and adored everywhere they went.

Life for these very capable women in the heart of Columbia's Old Shandon neighborhood was fun and safe.

Chapter 7

BLESSINGS IN ORANGEBURG

*Through many dangers, toils, and snares,
I have already come;
'tis grace hath brought me safe thus far,
and grace will lead me home.
"Amazing Grace"—John Newton (1779)*

Meanwhile, in Orangeburg, no one was sitting idle. The elation and excitement of the 2006 groundbreaking in Columbia had buoyed trustees' spirits, and they were ready to elevate the Orangeburg project to the next level. The words of the apostle Paul rang true: all things are possible through Christ who strengthens us (Philippians 4:13).

Team Orangeburg was intensely aware that even with a generous ninety-nine-year, one-dollar land lease with The Oaks, coming out of the Orangeburg soil with bricks and mortar would require substantial capital. With encouragement from Rev. James McGee, Bishop Mary Virginia Taylor, and The Oaks Board, Aldersgate trustees pursued innovative strategies.

That's when a new Aldersgate friend entered the scene and everything changed. Extensively experienced in real estate development, Harris Davis, also of Orangeburg, deftly guided Aldersgate toward Housing and Urban Development, or HUD. Using his development expertise and knowledge of HUD, Davis and Aldersgate engaged grant writer Renda Allen to prepare a grant soliciting from HUD the entire cost of home construction.

Davis's company, N&H Enterprises, partnered with Allen and also with the Orangeburg County Disabilities and Special Needs Board to painstakingly compile the

Members of the women's tennis team at Orangeburg Preparatory School organized a successful tennis tournament to help build an Aldersgate home in Orangeburg. Above left is Louise Wannamaker. Above right are Laura McLachlan, Emily Black, Anne Griffin Patterson, and Ragan McDonald.

HUD grant and navigate the submission process. The grant was approved and awarded, and by the spring of 2007, Aldersgate had the resources in hand to start home number two.

Board member Daly Ward commented in an interview, "Once again, God in his incomprehensible timing had placed the perfect person at the perfect moment squarely in our laps. Harris Davis was pivotal in the development of Aldersgate. He was always the consummate Christian gentleman and he cherished the Aldersgate ministry."

Emily Black and Anne Griffin Patterson won the women's doubles tennis tournament, which helped raise needed funds for Aldersgate.

Judy Weathers added, "Without Harris's help, we would not have been able to fund the construction of the home." Later, he went on to play a significant role in the success of Aldersgate as a trustee and board treasurer.

Davis died in 2018, but the HUD grant he secured created a lasting legacy of his mark on Aldersgate. Remarkably, the grant provided far more than just construction; in perpetuity HUD will fund utilities, maintenance, appliances, repairs, insurance, and more.

While the HUD grant was transformative, Aldersgate needed additional funds to furnish, equip, and staff the home; acquire a van for resident transport; and address other start-up expenses. Aldersgate would soon learn that many in the Orangeburg

Aldersgate at The Oaks in Orangeburg held its ribbon cutting March 12, 2009, only weeks after the Columbia Builders Care Home opened.

community wanted to be involved.

Louise Wannamaker was a rising senior at Orangeburg Preparatory Schools in the summer of 2006. Louise's big heart for service melted when she heard about the Aldersgate project. Eager to help, she turned to something she knew best: competitive tennis.

Wannamaker and other players from her high school's women's tennis team organized a highly successful tournament, raising more than ten thousand dollars over a two-year period. Local businesses were recruited to provide sponsorships, prizes, food, and refreshments.

In addition to the tennis tournament, other Orangeburg community groups rallied behind the very special home at The Oaks. Several churches including First Baptist Church of Orangeburg, Shady Grove United Methodist, and Union United Methodist were generously involved in funding specific needs from the home's "wish list." The Orangeburg Junior Service League, local garden clubs, and numerous individuals held fundraisers or made outright gifts.

God was very good to Aldersgate at The Oaks.

+ + +

After breaking ground in August 2007, the Orangeburg home was under way, led by architect Marshall Gardner and C.F. Evans Construction of Orangeburg. By the summer of 2008, it was time to recruit future occupants. One resident was confirmed early on, but five more bedrooms needed to be filled. Judy Weathers recalls filling the home "was more challenging than Columbia. Some parents weren't ready to commit to placing their loved ones in a home."

Another issue for many prospective families was financial. House operations required considerable staff, food, overhead, and more, generally costing around three thousand dollars per resident, per month. At this point in the ministry's young life, there was no mechanism to fund these expenses except directly from families of residents. Knowing the need for residential alternatives was acute statewide, Aldersgate turned to the South Carolina Department of Disabilities and Special Needs (DDSN) for guidance.

DDSN representative Hester Wannamaker was delighted to assist. Knowledgeable and energetic, Wannamaker found applicants and employed a tool called a residential waiver to fund the month-to-month living costs for residents. The Orangeburg home was quickly filled.

+ + +

On March 12, 2009, only weeks after the Columbia Builders Care Home opened, the Orangeburg home also celebrated a ribbon cutting. Shortly thereafter, Orangeburg's first resident, Edward Mason, moved in.

Above is one of the men's bedrooms at Aldersgate at The Oaks in Orangeburg.

Some of the men learned to ride a bicycle for the first time thanks to Aldersgate.

Residents of Aldersgate at The Oaks—Keebler, Edward, Chris, and Brian—enjoy some hangout time.

Being surrounded by new friends and loving staff fosters a strong sense of Christian community as the men strive to live independently.

There were actually two moves in the Mason family that month. While Edward was settling into his new Aldersgate home, his mother, Jeanette, was moving next door to The Oaks. Jeanette's progressive dementia meant that she was confronting the same dilemma many South Carolina families continue to face: The caregiver now needs care herself.

Relatives had worked for years to find solutions for Edward and Jeanette. For Claire Mason Freeman, the notion that she could place her brother and her mother on the same campus in the same community was too improbable to dare pray or hope for. Yet pray she did, and blessings flowed.

"This has truly been a miracle because we looked for years to find a place where they could be together. Before today, there weren't any facilities a parent and a child could both go," Claire recalled.

Claire's husband, Edward Freeman, added that Aldersgate was "a real home" for his brother-in-law.

Surrounded by new friends, loving staff, and his mother only steps away, Edward Mason's years in an Aldersgate home were very happy.

Above, the men of Aldersgate at The Oaks enjoy a special dinner provided by Union UMC, Cope. Many churches volunteer to help the homes. Below, the men gather for a smile next to their new van.

Kathleen Baskin and Rev. Milton McGuirt break ground for Rick's House during a special ceremony March 3, 2014. The home was a partnership among Baskin, The Manor, and Aldersgate.

Chapter 8

GOD-SIZED DREAMS IN FLORENCE

Happy the home when God is there,
and love fills every breast;
when one their wish, and one their prayer,
and one their heavenly rest.
"Happy the Home When God Is There"—Henry Ware Jr. (1846)

With two homes fully operational for several years, Aldersgate was anxious to expand to another community. Trustees soon learned that they would not find home number three. Rather, the third Aldersgate home would find them.

It was 2013, and for nearly a century, Kathleen Baskin had led a rich, full life of generosity and service to God. Now living at The Manor in Florence, South Carolina, Baskin had long ago stopped counting birthdays and instead focused on her real passion: living abundantly and giving generously.

For years, Baskin had held a dream that a group home with a loving, Christian environment could be located in Florence. Rev. Ann Ayres, chaplain of The Manor, was the first to share with Baskin that United Methodist properties in the conference were allowing group homes to be built and operated for adults with special needs. A short time later she heard the same message when former chair Judy Weathers spoke at Baskin's church about the Aldersgate ministry.

Innately decisive, Baskin needed no further sign. She reached for her phone and called Betty Moss McGuirt, chair of the Aldersgate Board of Trustees.

Kathleen Baskin had an offer that could not be refused.

+ + +

On the other end of the telephone, McGuirt stood astonished. Earlier that very same day, Bishop L. Jonathan Holston had connected with her and others at the Annual Conference as he gently challenged attendees to develop "God-sized dreams." He seemed to be speaking directly to her. Now, only hours later, she was talking to a benefactor who would completely fund the construction of an Aldersgate home at Florence's The Manor.

In God's world there are no unexplained coincidences. We expect our petitions to be answered eventually in accordance with God's will and timing, but McGuirt's prayer had arrived on angel's wings by priority express!

The Florence project quickly gained traction. Baskin's daughter, Kathleen DeBerry Brungard, contacted John Orr, The Manor board chair, to propose the idea of The Manor providing land for a home in a similar fashion to Columbia and Orangeburg.

Orr and other Manor board members immediately embraced the plan: "This is a good fit for us. We have the land and Mrs. Baskin is a resident, so we felt it would be good outreach. We are glad we can help."

On March 3, 2014, the groundbreaking took place with a large crowd attending the celebration. Site work, infrastructure, and construction began almost immediately with architect Hal Fuller supervising. The house was completed in about a year, and a dedication was held on April 19, 2015, with Baskin present to cut the ribbon.

Kathleen Baskin (second from left) and her daughters Kathleen Brungard, Jacquelyn Odell and Maria Clayton smile after breaking ground on Rick's House. The home is named for Frederick "Rick" Howard DeBerry Jr., Baskin's special needs son who died when he was thirty.

Chapter 9

WHEN YOU PASS THROUGH THE WATERS, I WILL BE WITH YOU (ISAIAH 43:2)

*"When through the deep waters I call thee to go,
the rivers of woe shall not thee overflow;
for I will be with thee, thy troubles to bless,
and sanctify to thee thy deepest distress."*
"How Firm a Foundation"—John Rippon (1787)

Living in Columbia's Old Shandon community is highly desirable, but as the poet Henry Wadsworth Longfellow writes, "Into each life some rain must fall." Apparently, every one thousand years, a colossal amount of rain will fall.

On Sunday, October 4, 2015, a freakish rainstorm pounded the geographic center of the state with twenty-three inches of water in twenty-four hours. The South Carolina Midlands and especially the City of Columbia were unprepared for what became known as "The Thousand-Year Storm." Columbia's Builders Care Home, already situated in a low, natural basin between Devine Street and Millwood Avenue, was flooded with more than sixteen inches of storm water.

Aldersgate staff on duty that evening and six anxious residents watched cautiously as water slowly rose around the house and seeped under door thresholds. Thankful for flood drills and emergency training, staff knew intuitively that even if the rain stopped soon, the water would continue to rise.

Cooperatively and without panic, staff and residents fled to the nearby home of the Epworth president. As they sloshed their way to higher ground, one of the residents remembered that water was spilling into her knee-high rain boots. They would later learn that water eventually cascaded over windowsills, lifting and floating

The Columbia house before (above) and after (below) the flood. The flooded home took eight months to reconstruct.

furniture and personal belongings.

All evacuated safely with no physical injuries, but there was extensive damage to the Builders Care structure. A beloved home for six women for more than five years was suddenly uninhabitable, and most of their personal possessions were ruined. Former trustee Caroline Stephenson explained that it was "sad to see everything they had worked hard to build being flooded away."

Betty Moss McGuirt, Aldersgate chair, had the difficult task of contacting parents and sharing the news about the condition of the home.

Water from the devastating flood cascaded over windowsills, lifting and floating furniture and personal belongings.

McGuirt explained, "Most of the parents lived in the Columbia area and were already aware of the status of the house. We were thankful for the safety of residents and staff, but it was a very sad day for all."

Families had no choice but to bring their daughters back to their parental homes and wait for the next step. Stephenson added that it was especially hard on residents because they had grown close to one another and were very comfortable in their routines together.

"They were devastated and missed each other terribly," she recalled.

Not long after the shock of losing the Columbia home, a new sadness gripped the displaced women of the Builders Care Home. Staff and parents compared notes and reported a common symptom to Chair McGuirt: The residents were homesick, missed each other, and needed to be back together.

Once again, Epworth came through. McGuirt met with Rev. John Holler, Epworth president and CEO, and particulars were quickly settled. She recalls Epworth "literally opening their doors" by providing housing while the home was being rebuilt. Back together again on the Epworth campus, the residents were elated to resume their routines under the same roof.

It took eight months to renovate the Builders Care home. McGuirt and her husband, Rev. Milton McGuirt, led the effort, consulting with builders and securing the capital for reconstruction while facing stringent new requirements for enhanced flood control.

The price tag of more than $300,000 included repairs, renovations, a water suppression system surrounding the home, two generators for emergency power, and extensive storm water drainage improvements. Inspections and approvals eventually followed from the Department of Health and Environmental Control, city code

After the flood, the residents had to move back in with their parents temporarily. But homesick, they desperately missed each other and needed to be back together. Epworth Children's Home opened its doors, providing housing while their Aldersgate home was being rebuilt.

officials, the Department of Disabilities and Special Needs, and insurance underwriters. After eight arduous months, on May 28, 2016, the residents were finally able to return to the home they had grown to love as their own and were elated to be reunited in a freshly refurbished house.

Stephenson commented that with the new flood control measures in place, "If the next great flood comes to Columbia, the one dry place will be the Builders Care Home in Shandon!"

Several of the residents agreed that the improvements made them feel safe and very secure.

Chapter 10

RICK'S HOUSE: CELEBRATING ABILITIES

Love divine, all loves excelling,
joy of heaven to earth come down;
fix in us thy humble dwelling;
all thy faithful mercies crown!
"Love Divine, All Loves Excelling"—*Charles Wesley (1747)*

Naturally philanthropic and enterprising, Kathleen Baskin was bringing the vision of a Florence home to fruition. She loved the Aldersgate model and especially that God's hand was in all facets of the ministry, but Baskin had another very personal reason for her heart to swell with gladness as the Florence home progressed.

Her only son, Frederick "Rick" Howard DeBerry Jr., was born in 1944 with multiple disabilities. By age thirteen he was also blind. Adored by his family, Rick pushed his handicaps aside as best he could and enjoyed life to the fullest as an outgoing young man.

A close family, Rick's sisters, Maria, Kathy, and Jacquelyn, always helped with their brother's needs.

"He went everywhere we went. He even learned to ride a bike," said Maria, Rick's youngest sister. "I think I have a nurturing personality now because of him. It taught me patience and perseverance."

Middle sister Jacquelyn Odell said the unfortunate part about her brother did not lie in his disabilities but in people not focusing on his abilities.

Echoing Jacquelyn's comments, her mother added, "He was a really smart man. Unfortunately, the normal person meeting him wouldn't know that. I was amazed at what he could do with his abilities."

Aldersgate Special Needs Ministry dedicated its newest home, Rick's House (above), June 2015 on the campus of The Manor in Florence.

Three of the residents of Rick's House enjoy a game of UNO.

The homes provide a Christian environment and friends who become much like brothers.

Rick died in 1974 at the age of thirty.

"He lived ten years past his father, and it made me think how handicapped people can outlive their parents," said his mother as she reflected on the importance and relevance of the Aldersgate mission. "Sometimes they don't have siblings or other family members who can take care of them."

Rick's House was jubilantly opened March 7, 2016, to serve four men with developmental disabilities. The first resident was Franz Hicks, son of retired United Methodist minister and former Aldersgate trustee the Rev. Granville Hicks. Other residents soon followed, and within months the house was filled.

Chapter 11

CUTTING THE APRON STRINGS

*Now thank we all our God,
with heart and hands and voices,
who wondrous things has done,
in whom this world rejoices.*
"Now Thank We All Our God"—Martin Rinkart (1636)

By 2018, trustees had piloted Aldersgate, with God always by their side, for more than sixteen years as a volunteer-only organization. Many executive committee members have remarked that Aldersgate is among the most beloved causes they ever served—but also one of the most demanding.

With numerous employees in every home, ever-changing regulations, new licensure requirements, expanding development demands, and the strong desire to add more homes, it was time for trustees to relinquish day-to-day duties and find a professional to take the management helm.

An extensive search yielded numerous qualified candidates, but one in particular caught the attention of the personnel committee, which was steered by board chair Sam Waldrep and future board chair Susan Kovas. Elaine G. Mathis came to Aldersgate in spring 2018 with two decades of nonprofit management experience.

Mathis was quoted in the June 2018 issue of the *South Carolina United Methodist Advocate* as saying, "I look forward to applying my experience in my new role and helping advance Aldersgate's impactful mission."

+ + +

Elaine G. Mathis (above) came to Aldersgate as executive director in spring 2018 with two decades of nonprofit management experience. Below, residents Margaret Brabham, Bryant Shelley, and Damon Campbell share what Aldersgate Special Needs Ministry means to them at the 2019 annual meeting.

Shortly after Mathis's arrival, the board entered a challenging period that saw the addition of new homes stymied by government agencies. Sweeping changes to Medicaid waiver guidelines deeply affected the ministry's ability to open new group homes in South Carolina. Despite the great need statewide, Medicaid funds were not

Independent living fosters confidence and joy in the residents.

Damon shows off his gardening talents, one of the independent skills he hones in his new home.

available for Aldersgate's typical six-bed format. Mathis spent considerable time with the South Carolina Department of Disabilities and Special Needs, working diligently to understand and navigate the new regulations.

With efforts to open more facilities in the immediate future now legislatively thwarted, Aldersgate leadership was determined to continue moving forward in a productive way. Waldrep was a passionate believer in comprehensive strategic planning and immediately realized a long-term plan was not in place. Waldrep guided trustees very ably as this process for a long-term plan was set in motion.

In 2019, Dan Holloway of Pinnacle Leadership Associates was selected to facilitate several board and management tactical sessions over a period of nearly a year. These gatherings led to new and creative avenues of service in the form of defined work groups.

The Grassroots Coalition and Advocacy Group was one example, created for the purpose of placing an Aldersgate advocate in each of the twelve districts in the South Carolina Conference. Rev. Steve Patterson, Aldersgate trustee and superintendent of the Anderson District, helped write the group guidelines. Patterson launched the pilot advocacy program in the Anderson District along with Dr. Sandra Stevens-Poirel, superintendent of the Charleston District.

Others such as Carolyn Briscoe, a ministry assistant at a Clemson, South Caro-

Residents of Aldersgate at The Oaks enjoy some quality time together.

During a rare South Carolina snowfall, a resident makes a snow angel. Residents make plenty of time for joy each day.

Local churches pitch in to help with the home's needs. Here, Washington Street's Drive-n-Drop collects paper goods for Aldersgate.

lina, church, enthusiastically embraced the advocacy effort. Briscoe methodically contacted each United Methodist pastor in the Anderson District, sending them Aldersgate materials and urging support for the ministry. Comfortable as a public speaker, Briscoe shared her passion for Aldersgate in many Upstate churches. As a result, Aldersgate saw a significant spike in interest in the ministry as well as an

The women are much like sisters. Here, they enjoy a day out on the town.

Aldersgate residents spend some time at the Columbia Fireflies baseball game.

increase in giving from the Anderson District. Fulfilling another component of the advocacy work group's objectives, members regularly contacted legislators and participated in Disability Advocacy Day at the South Carolina Statehouse.

A New Homes Group was formed during this time for the purpose of identifying possible home site locations when construction could once again move forward. This group also investigated innovative residential business models and housing systems. Over the course of the next year, the New Homes Group traveled and observed housing trends in places such as Osprey Village in the South Carolina Lowcountry; Friendship Houses of Reality Ministries of Durham, North Carolina; and other planned neighborhoods.

Private Providers Group was founded to meet and share ideas with experienced residential operators already established in South Carolina. Private Providers recruited several credentialed professionals including Bob Kearns of the Presbyterian Agency for the Developmentally Disabled and Sarah Pope, CEO of SOS Care, South Carolina, a nonprofit organization currently building Oak Tree Farm, a residential community for autistic and intellectually disabled adults in Conway, South Carolina.

Additional participants were W.C. Hoecke of Harmony Christian Community, a planned neighborhood for the Columbia area; Diane Wilush, CEO of United Cerebral Palsy of South Carolina; Lindsey Daniel, state director of Community Options, Inc.; and Lorri Unumb, attorney and a nationwide leader in autism advocacy, insurance law reform, and residential options for special needs adults.

This stellar collection of leaders exchanged ideas and discussed how to survive the constantly morphing licensure and political climate.

Chapter 12

MAN PLANS ... GOD SMILES

*Then let the world give up its rage,
nor put a church in fear;
let lives be lived through every age
in the Almighty's care.*
"Give Thanks to God, Invoke His Name"—*Isaac Watts (1719)*

In the opening days of January 2020, Aldersgate trustees were brimming with optimism. Skillful administrator Linda Gifford had just joined Elaine Mathis on staff; highly beneficial long-term planning strategies had been adopted; work groups were a success; and best of all, a new report had just emerged indicating Medicaid funding for new homes would soon be allocated to South Carolina.

It seemed absolutely certain that Aldersgate expansion would begin again very soon. Surely nothing would detour this new momentum.

Man plans ... God smiles.

A few short weeks into 2020, a mysterious virus impacted every country, every community, and every organization across the globe, including and especially Aldersgate.

COVID-19 was upon us.

Aldersgate priorities immediately shifted from home expansion to resident and staff safety. A period of intense stress and concern followed as management and staff made their way through an uncharted sea of sanitation protocols, safety policy development, desperate searches for personal protective equipment, and other challenges that seemed to appear anew on a daily basis. All this occurred while staff simultaneously helped residents comprehend a new normal, one that limited access to family

A Washington Street UMC member unloads donations of water for the Aldersgate homes during the pandemic. COVID-19 brought new challenges for the ministry.

and staff and ended many of their beloved activities.

Advocacy efforts begun only months before the start of the pandemic proved beneficial. Legislators, with whom Aldersgate had developed a close rapport, responded quickly to the need for assistance, such as safety policies for residents.

Despite prodigious efforts to prevent exposure, several residents contracted COVID. All received excellent medical care and managed to return to their Aldersgate homes without complication. As soon as the vaccine was available, management worked to make Aldersgate residents and staff among the first to obtain access.

As "social distancing" quickly became a part of the pandemic's worldwide lexicon, Aldersgate learned that a simple but spacious screened porch can be the ideal place to bring folks together peacefully and safely.

"We will never build another home without one!" Susan Kovas remarked.

+ + +

Outdoor socializing helped a great deal during the pandemic.

University of South Carolina journalism student Mimi Sizemore collected interviews during summer 2021 to make this book possible.

Residents like Damon, pictured, learned to live with a new normal during the pandemic, one that limited access to family and staff and ended many of their beloved activities.

Both a pandemic and an unfavorable regulatory environment now obstructed development. Undeterred, the board considered fresh ways to grow Aldersgate and expand the ministry.

One such opportunity emerged from the work group portion of strategic planning. Trustees had long known that weary caregivers needed an occasional pause from their unending responsibilities, if only for a few hours. But options in the Midlands were limited. The Respite Services work group was charged with studying forms of respite for caregivers of adults with special needs.

University of South Carolina students pursuing Master of Social Work degrees were engaged to research the possible need for respite services. Pleased to be getting real world experience, the students held separate focus groups for social work case managers and caregivers. Students concluded the need for respite care was substantial and acute.

After hearing these reports and studying other programs around the state, trustees voted unanimously in 2021 to launch a respite ministry. Aldersgate in the Morning, or AIM, was founded in partnership with Grace United Methodist Church in the Harbison area of Columbia. A director was hired and volunteers were trained. Grace agreed to share their childcare facilities with AIM for a two-day-a-week respite

Above, residents enjoy a Fireflies minor league baseball game during the pandemic. Below, the women accept a donation on Aldersgate Sunday, held in spite of COVID-19.

program for caregivers. AIM gave caregivers a break while adults with special needs gained a fun place to enjoy each other socially.

Unfortunately, several elements did not come together. The pandemic was still lingering; volunteers were hard to secure and retain; and identifying program coordinators and clients was difficult. After a year, AIM was closed. While this allowed Aldersgate to refocus on its true mission to open homes, the closure was a disappointment. However, a model was created that could be used for the future.

Despite prodigious efforts to prevent exposure, several residents contracted COVID. All received excellent medical care and managed to return to their Aldersgate homes without complication.

God's abundantly beautiful South Carolina outdoors presented another unique opportunity in late 2021. Arthur Spriggs, executive director of United Methodist Camps and Retreat Ministries for South Carolina, began work on a summer camp experience for Aldersgate residents. In time for the summer sessions of 2022, the program was a reality.

Held at Asbury Hills Camps and Retreat Center in Cleveland, South Carolina, the camp provided residents with adventures in canoeing, archery, camp songs, bunking in rustic cabins, dining hall meals, and full absorption into the splendor of God's great outdoor world. Of course, no summer camp outing is complete without a glowing campfire and one too many s'mores!

Residents enjoyed the Asbury Hills experience so much in 2022 and 2023 that the ministry plans to continue this as an annual summertime pilgrimage.

Linda, Margaret, and Callie do some canoeing at the UMC's Asbury Hills Camps and Retreat Center in Cleveland, South Carolina, which gave residents the chance to bask in God's creation.

Chapter 13

TURNING POINT

"Awake, O sleeper, and arise ..."
—Ephesians 5:14 (ESV)

In early 2022, Aldersgate and the rest of the world were finally emerging from the pandemic's two-year dark cloud. Trustees were jubilant that the February 2022 Aldersgate Annual Meeting would be in person, not virtual, and held at The Oaks in Orangeburg. Elaine Mathis secured a strong slate of speakers, including attorney Lorri Unumb and Dr. Michelle Fry, executive director of the South Carolina Department of Disabilities and Special Needs. Lori Manos, associate state director of policy with the same agency, also addressed the well-attended meeting.

Something subtle in Fry's and Manos's remarks piqued the attention of Mathis and other trained listeners in the audience that day. A review of the meeting transcript confirmed highly encouraging news that a shift in funding policy was possibly forthcoming. If true, this would allow home construction finally to resume for those on the state's critical needs list.

Only weeks later, on March 2, 2022, Aldersgate participated in South Carolina Disability Advocacy Day at the South Carolina Statehouse. Mathis and Susan Kovas met with State Sen. Mike Fanning of District 17 (Chester, Fairfield, and York counties). As a longtime resident of District 17 and friend of Senator Fanning, Kovas knew the experienced senator would listen and take action. He began placing phone calls immediately. Soon after, Senator Fanning would take other steps, providing detailed information on social media about Aldersgate and the dearth of special needs housing. Gears long seized from inactivity began to move again.

These events were a turning point in the exciting new era of Aldersgate's expansion.

Callie, Cameron, and Boyd (above) speak at the 2022 Annual Meeting about living in Aldersgate homes.

Sen. Mike Fanning meets with Aldersgate supporters who want to increase housing for adults with special needs.

Emma DeVenny of the Arras Foundation, Rev. Joseph Kovas, and Grant Kovas advocate for housing for adults with disabilities during Disability Advocacy Day on the Statehouse Lawn. Below, the turnout was impressive.

+ + +

After four years as executive director, Mathis left Aldersgate in spring 2022 to accept a new position. She had successfully led a new era in Aldersgate's management structure, administration, and governance, making it possible for trustees to step back from day-to-day responsibilities and function in more traditional board roles. Under her leadership, Aldersgate survived a historic pandemic, created a newslet-

The ladies from the Columbia Builders Care Home participate in the 2022 Disability Advocacy Day at the Statehouse.

In 2022, Kim Thomas was hired as executive director and brought with her more than twenty years of management experience.

ter, uncovered avenues for new home construction, significantly increased funding for the Builders Care home through Midlands Gives, and experienced substantial increases in giving from conference churches on Aldersgate Sunday.

Aldersgate employees, residents, and trustees remember Mathis affectionately as an effective communicator and a gracious, professional leader.

Shortly after Mathis' departure, Kim Thomas was hired as executive director and brought with her more than twenty years of highly relevant management experience. Her impressive credentials included a role as president/CEO for the South Carolina Autism Society. She also held positions with the Whitten Center Department of Disabilities and Special Needs, Fairfield County Disability and Special Needs Board, Tri-County Development in Aiken, South Carolina, as well as experience with fundraising and legislative advocacy.

In addition, Thomas has been a key member of several state-level advisory groups with the Department of Disabilities and Special Needs, Vocational Rehabilitation, and the Department of Education.

Past Chair Kovas and 2022 Chair W. C. Hammett shared that Thomas stood out above all the other applicants. Another executive committee member commented, "We are thrilled to have someone of Kim's caliber leading Aldersgate. She has been an exceptional executive and elevates the ministry with every new initiative she brings to our organization. She has excellent comprehension of our vision and mission, and we are fortunate to have her in the executive director's role."

Executive Director Kim Thomas and Xavier practice archery at Asbury Hills in August 2023.

Chapter 14

2023: ALDERSGATE TODAY

I sing a song of the saints of God, patient and brave and true.
"I Sing a Song of the Saints of God"—Lesbia Scott (1929)

The state of Aldersgate Special Needs Ministry is more vibrant and robust than it has ever been.

God's abundant love has been revealed in Aldersgate's growth and in his provision of outstanding employees and home staff who are at the core of the ministry's success. With low staff turnover and high devotion to the needs of the men and women who call Aldersgate home, it is not unusual for residents to develop close ties to staff members.

In 2023, the first three Aldersgate homes continue to prosper.

Six women reside in the Columbia Builders Care home. When asked what is the best part about their home, their response is always the same: loving, caring staff. Indeed, the Columbia house family has always been much more than six residents. Skilled employees nurture every resident to help her reach her highest, fullest potential. With a focus on achieving self-reliance, many residents are able to hold meaningful jobs.

It is no surprise that the women of the Builders Care home are very active in their community. They attend church and volunteer for events at Epworth Children's Home. A Columbia parent observed that Aldersgate keeps her daughter busy and engaged: "Aldersgate was the best thing that could have happened to my daughter because it has provided her with a loving Christian home where she can learn to be independent."

Aldersgate at The Oaks hosts six men, and like the Builders Care home, they are

Aldersgate at The Oaks hosts six men as of 2023.

Aldersgate at The Oaks men often enjoy watching sports together, especially when it involves a friendly rivalry between the Clemson Tigers and South Carolina Gamecocks.

supported by an exceptional staff. These employees are like family to the residents. One of the men lost multiple loved ones in the span of a year and was very expressive about the comfort and support he received from staff.

The crew also works to build residents' life skills such as cooking, home care, and laundry. Busy with a variety of activities, the men take walks in a nearby park, visit

Rick's House hosted a barbecue lunch in June 2023 for members of the South Carolina United Methodist Annual Conference, where people got to learn more about Aldersgate Special Needs Ministry.

At left, residents chat on the rocking chairs outside Rick's House, located at The Manor in Florence. At right, Kathleen Baskin, who died in November 2023, was overjoyed that Aldersgate honored the memory of her son by providing a loving home in Rick's name.

the library, and go on community outings. At the home, residents enjoy watching sports together, especially when it involves a friendly rivalry between the Clemson Tigers and South Carolina Gamecocks.

Rick's House in Florence is flourishing and serving the community. Kathleen Baskin, who died in November 2023, was overjoyed that Aldersgate honored the memory of her son by providing a loving home in Rick's name. Baskin remained involved with Rick's House until her death and visited frequently, often indulging residents with favorite treats and snacks.

The immensely pivotal 2022 meeting with Senator Fanning allowed new home openings to begin again. As a result, Tommy's House became the ministry's fourth home. Nestled in a quiet Columbia neighborhood, this existing house was purchased in spring 2023. After a few minor improvements, it was dedicated on September 13, 2023, with past chair Rev. Stephen Taylor presiding. A home for men, Tommy's House is named in memory of the younger brother of Rev. Milton McGuirt, beloved Aldersgate trustee emeritus.

Tommy McGuirt had profound special needs, but far more significant was the exceptional bond between Tommy and his big brother, Milton. Tommy inspired Milton's career in ministry as well as his lifelong passion for helping the disabled. When he was born, Tommy was not expected to live into his teenage years. His full, abundant, sixty-four-year life is further evidence that God is in control and amplifies the urgency of Aldersgate's role in providing for those who outlive their caregivers. Rev. McGuirt and his wife, Betty Moss, have been tireless supporters and leaders of the Aldersgate ministry.

Soon after Kim Thomas became executive director, she pursued the possibility of a second home on the campus of The Manor in Florence. Thanks to her tenacity and The Manor leadership, a groundbreaking for a new Florence home was held on

The Rev. Milton and Betty Moss McGuirt are longtime supporters of Aldersgate Special Needs Ministry.

A home for men, Tommy's House (above) is named in memory of the younger brother of the Rev. Milton McGuirt.

Residents and supporters break ground on Aldersgate's home number five, Sunshine House

March 12, 2023, with Rev. Steve Patterson presiding. Home number five, Sunshine House, is a residence for men and will be ready for occupancy in late 2023 or early 2024.

In proximity to each other, the two Florence homes are similar in two striking ways: First, they share the same handsome design and efficient floor plan. And second, like Rick's House, the construction of Sunshine House was also completely funded by a generous donor cultivated by Thomas. God is good!

Chapter 15

ALDERSGATE TOMORROW

*Be Thou and Thou only
the first in my heart
O High King of heaven,
my Treasure Thou art.
"Be Thou My Vision"—Mary F. Byrne, trans. (1905)*

As God's plan for Aldersgate continues to reveal a bright and promising future, homes six, seven, eight, and many more feel close at hand.

From the very beginning, Aldersgate founders and trustees have been led and inspired by God's word as found in Isaiah 32:18: "My people will live in peaceful dwelling places, in secure homes, in undisturbed places of rest" (NIV).

Only God knows precisely what lies ahead for the Aldersgate journey. But as this beloved ministry looks to the next unwritten chapter, it remains Christ-led and profoundly focused on the mission to care for those who cannot care for themselves, while bringing peace and comfort to families and caregivers.

Aldersgate is graciously guided by an unchanging Savior in a challenging, ever-changing world.

Long-serving trustees the Rev. Milton and Betty Moss McGuirt capture the spirit of the ministry best when they are often heard to say, "The need is great! The task is great! Our God is greater!"

Together, the residents of Aldersgate homes are thriving and living their best lives.

Christmas is always merry for the women of the Columbia Builders Care Home.

About funding

Aldersgate does not receive apportionment funding from the South Carolina Conference of The United Methodist Church.

The conference has set aside the second Sunday of August to allow United Methodist churches the opportunity to offer support. Contributions from Aldersgate Special Needs Sunday help provide for the future of the ministry, but considerably more funding is needed for Aldersgate to continue to grow in God's kingdom.

It is anticipated that in the years to come, Aldersgate's base of support will expand within the broader Christian community. The need touches all peoples, all faiths, and all denominations.

To learn more: https://aldersgatesnm.org.

Help Us Grow

Chairs of Aldersgate Special Needs Ministry

Judy Weathers (2003-2008)
Rev. Stephen Taylor (2008-2010)
Betty Moss McGuirt (2010-2018)
Sam Waldrep (2018-2020)
Susan Kovas (2020-2022)
W. C. Hammett (2022-)

Acknowledgements and Resources

We wish to acknowledge and thank the many individuals and sources who contributed time, participated in interviews, gave quotes, and provided specific memories to this compilation:

Nancy Ayers
Kathleen Baskin
Fred Berry
Jessica and Matt Brodie
Kathleen DeBerry Brungard
Maria DeBerry Clayton
Harris Davis
Claire and Edward Freeman
Linda Gifford
W. C. Hammett
Yvette and Rich Hering
Faye Jackson
Joseph D. Kovas
Elaine Mathis
Margaret and Lawrence McCleskey
Betty Moss and Milton McGuirt
Jacquelyn DeBerry Odell
Caroline Stephenson
Stephen Taylor
Kim Thomas
Sam Waldrep
Louise Wannamaker
Emily and Daly Ward
Judy and Arden Weathers
The United Methodist Hymnal
South Carolina United Methodist Advocate
Orangeburg Times & Democrat
The State
The Columbia Star
The Florence Morning News
Angel Notes newsletter
Corporate Minutes of Aldersgate trustee meetings
Staff and residents

www.ingramcontent.com/pod-product-compliance
Lightning Source LLC
Chambersburg PA
CBHW022121090426
42743CB00008B/951